The Halloween Book

Jane Bull

A Dorling Kindersley Book

Dorling DK Kindersley

LONDON, NEW YORK, SYDNEY, DELHI, PARIS, MUNICH and JOHANNESBURG

For Charlotte, Billy, and James

DESIGN • Jane Bull
TEXT • Penelope York
PHOTOGRAPHY • Andy Crawford
DESIGN ASSISTANCE • Claire Penny

MANAGING EDITOR • Mary Ling
MANAGING ART EDITOR • Rachael Foster
DTP DESIGNER • Almudena Díaz
PRODUCTION • Orla Creegan
JACKET DESIGN • Andrew Nash

Published in the United States by
Dorling Kindersley Publishing, Inc.
95 Madison Avenue
New York, New York 10016

First American Edition, 2000
2 4 6 8 10 9 7 5 3 1

Library of Congress Catalog Card Number
00-026392

ISBN: 0-7894-6655-4

Color reproduction by GRB Edrice S.r.l., Verona, Italy
Printed and bound in Italy by L.E.G.O.

See our complete
catalog at
www.dk.com

Filled with Halloween magic.

Within this spooky book . . .

Lights and Decorations

Dressing Up

Party Time

Cackling Jack-o'-lanterns

Keep away grumbling ghouls, sinister spirits, and ghastly ghosts on Halloween night by positioning your jack-o'-lantern in a window. Dim the room, light the candles, and watch the cackling face flickering in the eerie darkness!

4

Where ghosts and demons flee with chilling, flickering faces in your windows

HOW TO MAKE FLICKERING FACES

Take the biggest, smoothest pumpkin you can find and carve this fantastic, jeering jack-o'lantern to warn wandering Halloween souls to keep well away from your house on the spookiest night of the year.

PEN

KNIFE

SPOON

BOWL

CANDLE

1 Take a knife and chop off its head

2 Gouge out the inside

Spook to you soon!

☻ Turnip Head

There are lots of different vegetables you can use. Why not try slicing a turnip face, which is what was used in Ireland – where the jack-o'-lantern originated. Watch out when you carve, however, turnips are tough!

☻ Candle Magic

Faces make very effective warnings, but decorative patterns look great too. Place a candle inside, light it carefully, pop the lid back on, and watch it twinkle in the darkness!

Ask an adult ...
☻ to help you cut the pumpkin
☻ to light the candle

3

Draw a face with jagged teeth

4

Cut out its eyes

Silhouette Windows

Swooping bats and petrified pumpkins silhouetted in your windows will startle any passerby!

Tape the tissue paper to the back of your picture.

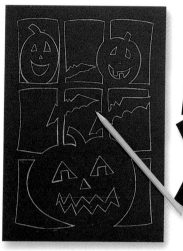

Draw a picture

Cut it out

Tape on tissue paper

👽 Creepy Castle

The lights are on in this castle, but is anyone at home? Create this creepy scene by using pieces of different colored tissue paper on the back of your picture.

Overlap the two ends and tape them to make the lampshade shape.

👽 Magic Lamp

You could even spook up a lamp. Measure and cut the shape of your lamp-shade out of black paper. Draw a Halloween picture on it, cut out the image, stick it onto your lamp, and turn on the light!

Flickering Flashlights

As dusk falls on Allhallows' eve it's time to create some shadowy light to guide the ghosts, spirits, and even yourself around your area. Jazz up your flashlight and decorate a jar to hang on a branch.

wend your way at witching hour in creepy candlelight

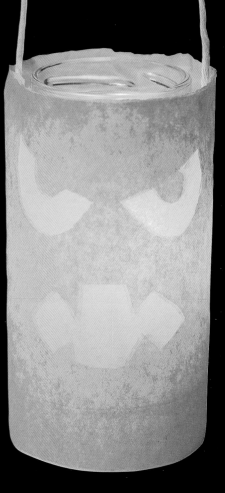

11

HOW TO MAKE JEERING JARS

Collect some glass jars or vases, any shape or size, and some bright tissue or plain tracing paper, and you are ready to start making your jeering jars and flickering flashlights! Small candles with flat bottoms are the safest candles to use and give a good flicker when placed inside your creepy jars. When you light them, make sure you ask someone to help you.

Ask an adult ...
to light the candle

Tissue Paper Face

A simple face is a great pattern to use. The candle shimmering through the features will drive off any wandering spirits!

Cut some tissue paper to fit the jar.

Draw a face and cut it out.

Tape the tissue to the jar.

Ask an adult to tie string securely around the rim, light a candle inside, and hang it up!

You could also add a layer of yellow tissue under the cutout face.

Night Jar

Another way to decorate a jar is to use tracing paper. Either use a marker to draw a picture on the paper, or cut out shapes from black card and stick them on. Wrap the paper around the jar and light the candle!

Cut out black shapes and stick them to the paper.

Draw a picture on the paper using a black marker.

Flashy Flashlight

Your friends will be green with envy when you flash your new light! Take it outside at dusk to see its full effect!

Cut tracing paper to fit around the flashlight with a 8-in. lengthwise.

Cut spooky shapes out of black paper and stick them on.

Wrap the paper around the end of the light with the shapes on the inside.

Tape down the seam.

Cut a frill out of crêpe paper and stick it around the handle.

Turn it on and you're ready to go!

13

Paper Chains

Screaming streamers are

easy to make and a perfect decoration to hang around a table or on a wall. Careful when you cut them, you don't want to separate your pumpkins or "nose to nose" cats!

Cut out a long strip of paper, 8 in. wide and however long you want, and fold it backward and forward in a square shape to make an accordion effect.

Folded edge

Folded edge

Folded edge

Draw your ghost design on the surface, making sure it runs to each folded edge.

Cut the ghost out leaving a part of the folded edges of each side uncut so that the ghosts are holding hands when you pull the paper apart.

Pull it out, decorate it, and hang it up!

Creepy Costumes

A witch's hat and nails can be bought from a local store.

Sew some black pointy ears onto a hairband.

Feather boas make great fur and tails.

A black T-shirt, black leggings, and some black gloves are a perfect and simple base for a cat costume.

Dressing up is one of the most exciting parts of Halloween. Search your home, use a little imagination to get creative, and presto! A prize-winning costume!

A witch's cat with wispy, white whiskers

Turn yourself white as a sheet!

Sew felt facial features on to a white sheet and make holes in them so that you can see.

Spooky gloves can be bought from a local store or created from rubber gloves.

A length of material draped around your head and shoulders gives a good zombie effect!

Face Value

Decorating your face with face paints or wearing a mask can make all the difference to your costume. Turn to pages 20-27 to find out how to add that extra something to your Halloween look.

Be a groaning, grumbling ghost!

HOW TO CREATE CREEPY COSTUMES

Simple costumes can sometimes be the most effective – you don't have to spend a lot of time or money making a fantastic Halloween outfit. Here are some great ideas to get you searching around your house for suitable objects to turn into a pumpkin fairy or a prize-winning pirate!

Cut a "skull and crossbones" shape out of paper and stick it on a hat.

Wearing a pumpkin mask and carrying a pumpkin bucket (see pages 26 and 30) is simple but effective.

Adapt a pixie outfit to create an orange pumpkin fairy.

Tie a scarf around your waist to keep your pants up. It also makes a good place to keep your cardboard sword.

Remember to put on your shoes before you go from house to house!

Add ribbons to your shoes to match the necklace, bracelets, and bows.

Design an outfit with whatever you can find!

Tie a scarf around your head as a bandana.

Collect together clothes, toys, and pieces of material to make up a spooky Halloween costume.

Rolled-up, loose pants with long socks make a great pirate outfit.

18

Try making a witch's hat out of thin, black cardboard.

Be a little monster with a purple monster mask (see page 26).

Decorate a hair-band as a pixie tiara.

Finish off the outfit with some painted flowers and tendrils.

A little black dress and striped tights are perfect for a witch.

Make cuffs out of thin cardboard and use jelly beans as cuff links!

A large piece of material draped over the shoulders makes a good vampire cape.

Make a matching treat bucket (see page 30).

Face paints and a prop are all you need for a quick and easy outfit.

Stick white, paper bone shapes onto a black T-shirt and add the skeleton mask (see page 25).

19

Fearsome Features

It's amazing how a touch of face paint can change you into a fully fanged vampire or a grinning witch's cat. Choose a suitable Halloween theme and challenge anyone to recognize you!

Shiver me timbers, give the pirate a treat!

HOW TO PAINT FEARSOME FACES

Face paints are easy to use, but you have to take your time doing them to get the best result. Try experimenting with some styles on paper and then persuade a friend to let you loose on their face! Warning – face paints can be messy; you should have some towels handy!

Pirate

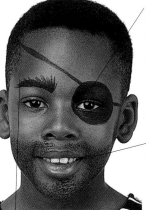

Paint a black eye patch around the eye and add a strap.

Use a coarse sponge to dab on some stubble.

Paint on a big, hairy eyebrow.

Draw some red scars and highlight them with white paint.

Scrunch up your face to help you to position the wrinkle lines.

Color in a black tooth with an eyeliner pencil.

Witch

Use a pale purple for the witch-like eye-shadow.

Rub the same purple onto your cheeks as blush.

Paint on black eyebrows and use eyeliner around your eyes.

Mix black paint with the eyeshadow for the lipstick.

Add a creepy-crawly or two if you like!

Skull

Wear a black hairband to frame the face.

Sponge on a white base color.

Paint big, black eye sockets.

Blend in some yellow paint to add to the bony look.

Color the nose in black paint; note the shape.

Draw some black cracks around the face.

Create a toothy mouth with thin, black lines.

Sponge for blending colors or covering large areas.

Paintbrush for drawing on fine lines.

Water-based face paint – colors can be mixed together.

Eyeliner pencil for blacking out teeth.

Watch out for skin allergies – test first

Glitter for an extra highlight.

Black Cat

Color around the eyes using white paint.

Use a sponge to dab white paint around the mouth and chin.

Paint the nose and bottom lip pink.

Color black around the white part of the eyes.

Brush black strokes around the mouth and all over the rest of the face.

Finish the face with some strokes of silver glitter.

Scaly Monster

Start by sponging some yellow paint in the center of the face.

Dab green around the yellow and spread it over the hairline.

Use red for the eyeshadow and to flare the nostrils.

Draw on the scales, the lips, and around the eyes with black paint.

Paint on some white fang shapes and highlight them in black.

Vampire

Slick back your hair using lots of hair gel.

Dab on white paint with a sponge.

Rub some gray around the eyes for a sunken look.

Dab some gray along the cheekbones to narrow the face.

Draw a hairline and paint it with black paint.

Paint gray around the eye sockets and add some red lines.

Color the lips and draw in some fangs dripping with red blood!

23

Paper Plate Faces

Send a chill down the spines of your neighbors when you go "trick or treating" by wearing these creepy masks made out of paper plates. Try a creepy cat, a petrified pumpkin, a wicked witch, or even a sinister skull!

Make a menacing mask from a plain paper plate

24

Face from a plate

Draw a face and cut it out

Add some spooky features

Attach on some elastic

Cut this mask off under the cat's nose.

Use the whole plate for the pumpkin face.

The face can be shaped by stapling in the chin.

DECORATING PAPER PLATE FACES

Quick to make, fun to wear – these paper plate masks can be worn plain or decorated. Use any decoration you like – glitter and sequins give a great eye-catching sparkle, and different colored paints bring monsters and pumpkins to life!

Transform yourself into a paper plate monster!

Draw on your witch features.

Make some markings where you will cut and shape the face.

Cut and shape some facial features.

Snip the markings at the top and bottom, fold them in, and staple them to give you a shape.

Paint the mask, then glue on some glitter using craft glue.

ACRYLIC PAINT

CRAFT GLUE

GLITTER

Pumpkin head

Use swirly green glitter around the edge.

Black cat

Decorate the cat with glitter and sequins.

Purple monster

This monster face has green glitter spots – design your own decoration for your plate mask.

Keep away from green, warty witches!

Add green hair by cutting out a long piece of crêpe paper and cutting it into strips. Tape the finished fringe inside the mask.

Wicked witch

The hair adds a lot to this warty witch. For a thicker head of hair simply add more crêpe tendrils to the back of the mask!

Buckets of Treats

At twilight when the sun sets and you go knocking on neighbors' doors, take this sturdy pumpkin bucket to carry your treats. Or if there is a knock on your door, provide a treat with a difference!

How to Make Treat Buckets

Pumpkin Pail

Create this pumpkin treat bucket to take with you when you go out. But remember to start making it before Halloween to let it dry in time!

Use wallpaper paste or a flour and water mix.

Spread vaseline on a balloon so that it doesn't stick to the paper at the end.

Paste at least five layers of newspaper on the balloon.

Let it dry for two days propped upright in a jar.

Paint the whole bucket a single color and leave it to dry.

When it is dry, pop the balloon.

Paste the rim of the bowl and fold extra strips of newspaper over the edge.

A perfect pail for your tasty treats!

Puncture two holes in each side of the bucket and thread a length of rope through them as a handle.

Paint a pumpkin face onto the side of the bucket in black paint.

Leaf and Star Bucket

For a container that can be made quickly, simply cover a bucket with crêpe paper and decorate it! You could stick some Halloween stickers on it as well.

Find a good sized bucket with a handle, and a large piece of crêpe paper.

Stand the bucket on the crêpe paper, fold the paper over the rim and secure it with tape.

Bind the handle with a long strip of crêpe paper and secure each end with tape.

Cut leaf or star shapes out of paper.

Tape the leaves to pipe cleaners to tie onto the handle.

Wrap the pipe cleaners around a pencil to create the swirly effect.

Halloween Stickers

Draw Halloween shapes on blank, sticky labels.

Color them in and stick them where you want!

Candy Cones

These candy cones are perfect for giving to those who turn up at your door wanting goodies. They would also be great to give to guests at the end of a Halloween party.

Take a piece of paper, about 8 in. square.

Fold one corner across the center as shown.

Fold the other corner over the fold and fix it down with glue stick.

Decorate with Halloween stickers.

Fold up the base and stick it down.

Beastly Buffet

You can't have any old food at a Halloween party. You need a hair-raising banquet to serve to your ravenous guests. Make sure your table is groaning with gruesome goodies and some really horrifying snacks!

Ferocious faces

Haunted cookies

Spider's legs and eyeball snacks

Creepy cupcakes

Savory Bites

You can create a soulful look with these downcast cucumber and olive eyes.

Send your guests into howls of delight with these pizza people and bread roll monsters! Vegetables such as peppers and olives are perfect for creating features, and the best thing is – they taste fantastic too!

Cut some carrots into some odd, monster ear shapes.

Perfect for famished fiends

Long green chives are perfect as spindly, monster legs!

A piece of salami makes a perfect slappy tongue!

A row of sweetcorn makes grizzly monster teeth!

👽 Monster Contest

There are many different monsters you can make with bread rolls. Why not hold a "monster contest" with your friends to see who can make the most unappetizing creature for your beastly banquet!

Cut a radish in half for some yucky, red eyes.

👽 Pizza People

Decorated, ghostly pizza crusts make delicious party snacks. Why not challenge your friends to try and make their own face on a pizza base?

A monster mouthful!

Cut the pizza crust to make shaped pizzas.

Make sure you use your favorite toppings – you want to enjoy your beastly bites!

Devour my gruesome sausage fingers!

👽 Finger Feast

Yuck! Dare your friends to chew on these gruesome nibbles! Make the fingers with a sausage and a piece of red pepper or tomato as a fingernail. Pierce them with a toothpick and poke them into a big squash or watermelon.

The tomato nails look like sharp talons on the ends of the fingers!

A tomato-flavored dip goes perfectly with your finger buffet!

Sweet Treats

Sweet dreams!

Sweet food normally looks so mouthwatering – not these creepy cupcakes! Who would want to eat a hairy spider or an eyeball? But if your guests dare to try these terrifying tidbits, they'll see how tasty they really ar

Fairy Cakes

(Makes 24 cakes)

4 oz (125 g) soft margarine
4 oz (125 g) superfine sugar
4 oz (125 g) self-rising flour
1 tsp baking powder
2 large eggs
1 tsp vanilla extract

Put all the ingredients into a bowl and beat with a wooden spoon until the mixture is soft and creamy.
Divide the mixture equally between the wrappers (about 1 tsp in each).
Cook for 18-20 minutes (375°F/190°C). Leave to cool before decorating.

Tubes of writing icing – perfect for fine, delicate patterns.

Weird shaped sweets as well as gummies are great for decoration.

Icing

11 oz (325 g) icing sugar
3 tbsp water
(or lemon/orange juice)

Add water to sifted icing sugar and mix to a soft consistency.

Look into my eyes, what can you see?

Wobbly Webs

Would you be tempted by a spider's web cupcake? Not me! But they look great on a Halloween table!

Cover the cake with icing.

Take a toothpick and gently drag lines from the center outward.

Draw swirls with an icing pen.

Bees and Bugs

Gummies are great as wobbly bodies, and licorice sticks make good spindly legs. Try your own designs with any candy that you have handy.

Make decorative bases for your cakes out of colored paper.

Red Eye

The eyeballs are made with a cherry and red coloring as veins!

37

Hanging Horrors

The beauty of making a cookie dough is that you can cut it into any cookie shapes you want, then make a hole in them, and hang them up! But don't expect them to be hanging un-nibbled for long!

👽 Cookie Mix

(makes 12-14 cookies)

8 oz (250 g) plain flour
5 oz (150 g) butter
3 oz (90 g) icing sugar
grated rind of half a lemon
1 tbsp milk

Put the sifted flour, icing sugar, and butter into a bowl and rub together with your fingers to make crumbs. Add the milk and the lemon rind and knead together to make dough. Chill for 20 minutes.

Cook for 15 minutes (325°F/160°C).

When the cookies are cooked and cooled, add some simple decoration with colored icing using an icing pen.

Draw some ghostly shapes on a piece of cardboard and cut them out.

Roll the dough to about quarter of an inch thick and cut around your stamps to make the shapes.

This is the actual size that the cookies should be. You could trace around this ghost as a guide.

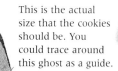

Put the cookies on a buttered baking sheet.

Pierce a hole in the top of each biscuit with a toothpick.

38

☻ Hanging Up

When the spooky cookies are ready, simply slip some thread through the hole and hang them up! They look just as good outside on branches as inside your home.

Swinging fiends as tasty tidbits

Cauldron

Pumpkin-head Punch bowl

What better way to serve delicious Halloween potions than inside a pumpkin cauldron! Carefully hollow out and carve a pumpkin in the same way as on page 6, mix the Apple Jack Fruit Punch on the next page, and serve it with a ladle!

Put the glass bowl into your punchbowl and fill it with your perfect punch.

Cocktails

Drinks to leave you shaken and stirred

are essential for every Halloween party. The idea is to alarm your friends with slimy, frothing, or vampire-blood colored drinks that taste as good as they look!

I dare you to try my blood-red potion!

Apple Jack
Fruit Punch

Mix this delicious fruit drink, perfect as a harvest punch, and serve it up in the pumpkin-head punch bowl. It will serve 10 very thirsty party-goers!

Fixing the Fruit

1 quart apple juice, 1 quart lemon-lime soda
Fruit: e.g. apples, tangerines, kiwi fruit.

Mix together the apple juice and lemon-lime soda. Add the small fruit whole and slice the larger fruit into pieces. Why don't you chop the apples or kiwi fruit into rings and cut them with a star-shaped cookie cutter?

41

How to Make Spooky Potions

These hair-raising potions can be made by the glass, as shown, or in large quantities for your pumpkin-head cauldron. You may need these ice techniques below.

Colored ice

Use colored juice or mix a few drops of food coloring into a jug of water, pour it into an ice tray, and pop it into a freezer overnight – simple but effective!

Crushed ice

To make the ice for your crushes, put some ice cubes into a bag, close the top, and whack it hard with a rolling pin!

Hot Chocolate Bones

Make this welcoming brew to warm the bones of the "trick or treaters" on their return!

Brewing the Bones

1 tsp of cocoa powder
1 mug of milk, some sugar, marshmallows

Mix a teaspoon of cocoa into a small amount of milk to make a paste, add some sugar to your taste, pour on hot milk, and stir it. Add the marshmallows, which will melt – delicious!

Decorate a long straw or spoon with a paper skull.

Lemon and Lime Slime

Watch the amazement on your friend's faces as the drink goes greener as the ice melts!

Slurping the Slime

1 glass of lemon-lime soda green ice cubes

Simply throw the ice cubes into the lemon-lime soda and decorate!

Hang a few creepy-crawlies from the side.

Candy Corn Crush

Try sucking this multi-colored crush up through a straw. You'll have to suck hard! If you can't, eat it with a spoon!

Combining the Crush

Crushed ice in three colors, use orange juice, cranberry juice, and plain water ice.

Crush the three colored ices and layer them on top of each other like a giant candy corn.

Make your own paper candy corn and stick it onto a spoon.

Vampire Broth

Mix this broth in front of your friends and watch it come alive before your eyes!

Fixing the Froth

1 glass of cola
1 scoop of vanilla ice cream

Fill a glass about two thirds full of cola, add a scoop of ice cream, and STAND BACK!

Cut out some black paper bats to swoop from your straws.

Witches Brew

Eye of newt, blood of bat, frog's tongue, and a squeeze of lemon. A brew with more than a few surprises!

Mixing the Magic

Half a cup of cranberry juice
Half a cup of lemon-lime soda
Green ice cubes
Gummy candy

Mix the cranberry juice and soda together, add the ice cubes and throw in the gummie candies as surprises!

Let a slithery, gummy snake slip over the side.

Fun and Games

Games are an essential part of a really good party – especially if you provide prizes for the winners. With these games you'd better give a prize to anyone who is willing to play them – only the bravest will want to!

Ghost train

All aboard the ghost express! Take your friends on a trip to trembling towers! Sit one person on a chair and blindfold them. Use sounds effects while running props past their face. Cold ice will give a sharp shock. Is that a hairy spider or is it just a feather?

Use your imagination and they will use theirs!

A jittery journey!

Plunge in Gunge

Mix together some really horrible gunge in a bucket. You could use a flour and water mix. The idea is that you can't see through it. Place some objects in the gunge and dare your friends to plunge their hands into it to retrieve them.

A prize for anyone brave enough to delve into the unknown!

Shadow Theater

Do you know any really chilling ghost stories that will scare the living daylights out of your friends? If so, then here's a way to bring them to life. Hang a white sheet up tightly across the doorway, making sure you have a dim light shining behind it.

Guaranteed to give your guests the goosebumps!

Tell your story and at the same time create shadowy actions behind the sheet. You could cut out shapes of large props from big pieces of paper, such as a pair of scissors or a hammer, to help the story along.

One dark and moonlit night . . .

Make sure you use plenty of sound effects to get everyone into the right mood!

Funny Feelings

Only the bravest of guests should get involved with this game! The idea is for each person to plunge their hands into boxes of nasty things that they can't see. YUCK! Cut a hole in a box, big enough to fit a hand through, and place a plate or bowl inside containing something yucky.

Try some wet spaghetti as worms or a peeled grape as an eyeball!

Warning – this game causes a lot of shrieks!

It's slimy, eugh!

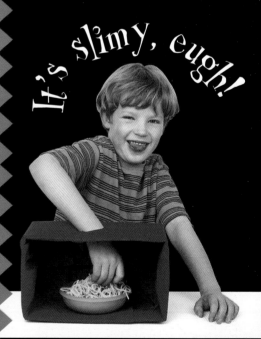

If you cut one side of the box away, then you can watch that the person really does put their hand in!

Apple Bobbing

Fill a bowl with water and drop a number of apples into it – you will find that they float on the surface. Each guest holds their hands behind their back while they try to remove an apple from the bowl using only their mouth. Anyone cheating is instantly disqualified and WATCH OUT – the floor can get pretty wet!

Dunk Crunch Splash

Dangling Doughnuts

Tie some doughnuts with pieces of string and hang them from a pole in a row. Tie each person's hands behind their backs, line them up to a doughnut, and MUNCH! The first to finish their doughnut is the winner. It's more tricky than it sounds and faces can get very messy!

Try hanging sugar doughnuts up, BUT one extra rule - no lip-licking!

Forfeits and Favors

Why not use home-made stickers to stick on the back of your pieces of paper?

A game of risk is always exciting to play. Fill a hat with pieces of paper, half with a forfeit written on them, and half with a name of a treat. Simply ask your friends to pick at their peril! Forfeits could include standing on your head or opening the front door and yelling "bananas!"

Treats could include extra candy or a small present

Pumpkin Seeds a Plenty

When you carve out your jack-o'-lanterns, you will find that you have a lot of seeds at the end. Well, don't throw them away. They are delicious to eat or can be threaded onto string as extra decoration or jewelry.

Roasted Pumpkin Seeds

8 oz (250 g) pumpkin seeds
2 tbsp vegetable oil
1 tsp salt

To roast your pumpkin seeds, first rinse them in water, then wrap them in a towel and pat them thoroughly dry. Put them in a large bowl and add the vegetable oil and salt. Lay them on a baking tray and cook for 12-15 minutes. (350°F/180°C).

Tie a knot in the end of the cotton before you thread on the seeds.

Thread them on to a piece of cotton to make necklaces and bracelets.

"TRICK OR TREAT" SAFETY

Remember ...

- always go out with an adult
- always go in a group
- only visit houses you know
- leave just after dark
- don't worry people who don't want to get into the spirit of Halloween

Secrets of success ...

- take a big bag – to fit lots of goodies!
- hint to your neighbors that you will be calling, you are likely to get more candy that way!

47

Index

Acknowledgments

With additional thanks to . . .
Emma Patmore for food styling
Stephanie Spyrakis for face painting
Charlotte Bull, Billy Bull, James Bull,
Tex Jones, Kiana Smith, Kristian Revelle, Maisie Armah,
and Elicia Edwards for being spooky models

Additional photography:
Dave King for the Turnip Head page 7, Gary Ombler for the witch
page 19, and Steve Shott for the witch pages 19, 33, 46.

48